CHRISTMAS FAVORITES

Solos and Band Arrangements
Correlated with Essential Elements Band Method

ARRANGED BY
MICHAEL SWEENEY

Welcome to Essential Elements Christmas Favorites! There are two versions of each holiday selection in this versatile book:
1. The SOLO version (with lyrics) appears on the left-hand page.
2. The FULL BAND arrangement appears on the right-hand page.

Use the optional accompaniment tape when playing solos for friends and family. Your director may also use the accompaniment tape in band rehearsals and concerts.

ISBN 978-0-7935-1758-9

HAL•LEONARD® CORPORATION
7777 W. BLUEMOUND RD. P.O. BOX 13819 MILWAUKEE, WI 53213

JINGLE BELLS

Words and Music by J. PIERPONT
Arranged by MICHAEL SWEENEY

Solo

Introduction

5

Jin - gle Bells,   Jin - gle Bells,   Jin - gle   all   the   way.

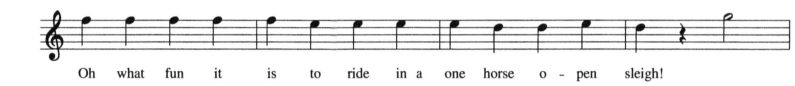

Oh   what   fun   it   is   to   ride   in   a   one   horse   o - pen   sleigh!

13

Jin - gle Bells,   Jin - gle Bells,   Jin - gle   all   the   way.

Oh   what   fun   it   is   to   ride   in   a   one   horse   o - pen   sleigh!

21 Interlude

Oh   what   fun   it   is   to   ride   in   a   one   horse   o - pen   sleigh!

JINGLE BELLS

Words and Music by J. PIERPONT
Arranged by MICHAEL SWEENEY

Band Arrangement

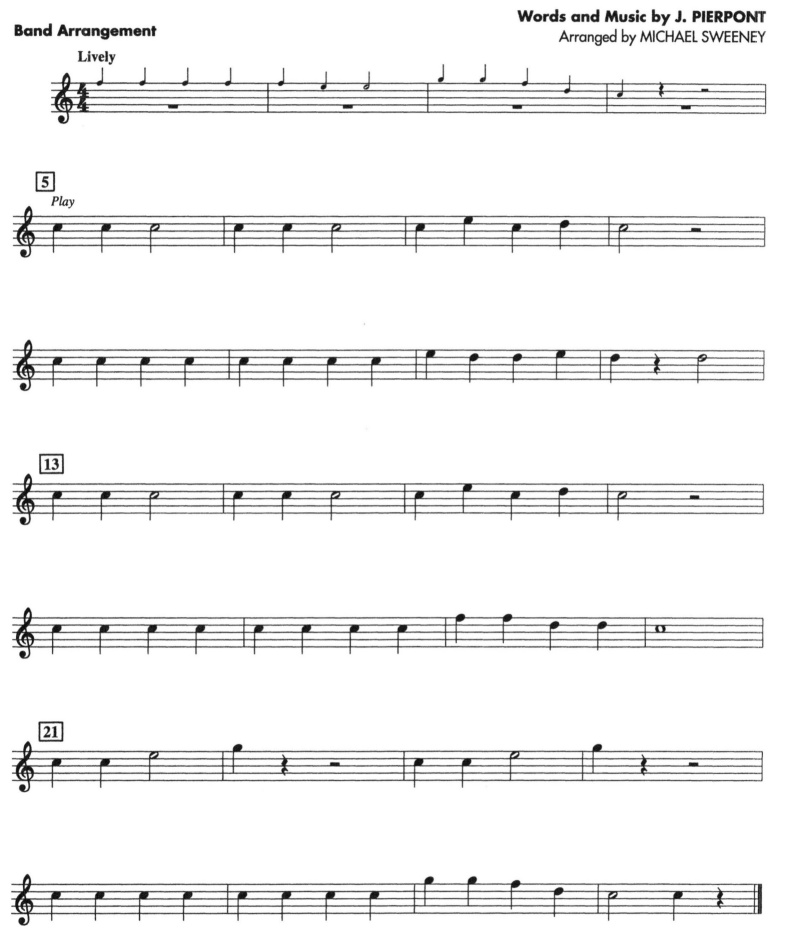

00862507

Arranged by MICHAEL SWEENEY

Solo

UP ON THE HOUSETOP

Band Arrangement

Arranged by MICHAEL SWEENEY

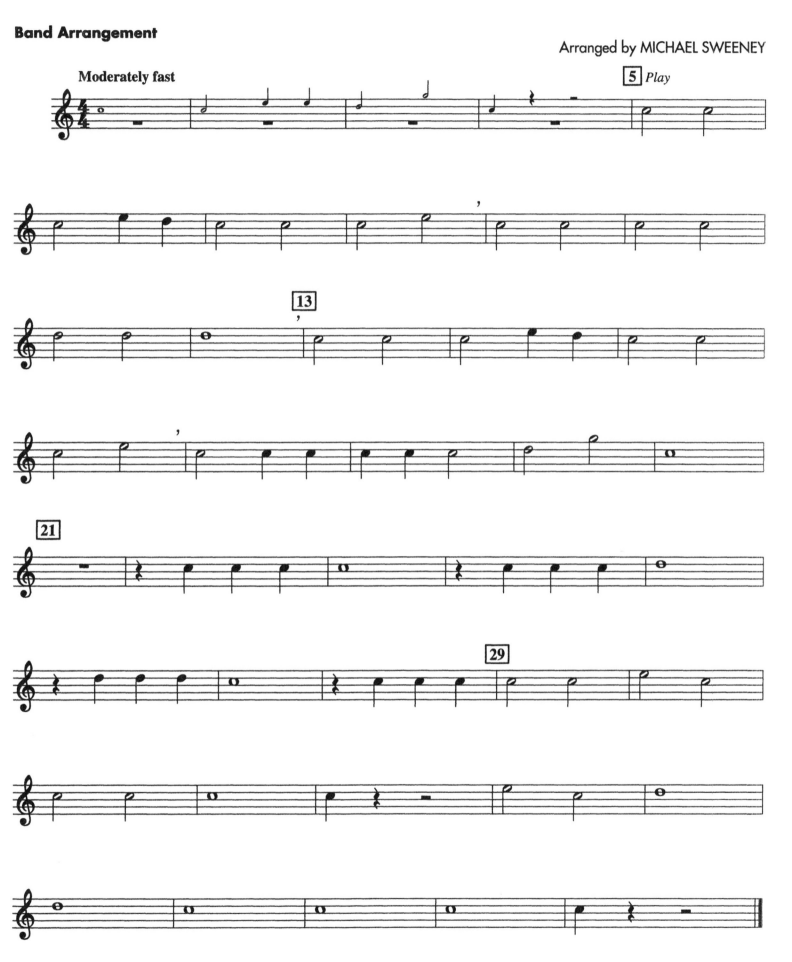

THE HANUKKA SONG

Arranged by MICHAEL SWEENEY

Solo

6

Lyrics:

Ha-nuk-kah, O Ha-nuk-kah, our voic-es are ring-ing. Ha-nuk-kah, we cel-e-brate with danc-ing and sing-ing. Chil-dren gath-er 'round now, and light up the lights. Mir-a-cles of old are with-in us to-night. The can-dles are glow-ing, the fes-ti-val now has be-gun. Come hear the sto-ry of God in His glo-ry and how no-ble free-dom was won. Ha-nuk-kah, O Ha-nuk-kah, our voic-es are ring-ing. Ha-nuk-kah, we cel-e-brate with danc-ing and sing-ing. Chil-dren gath-er 'round now, and light up the lights. Mir-a-cles of old are with-in us to-night. The can-dles are glow-ing, the fes-ti-val now has be-gun. Come hear the sto-ry of God in His glo-ry and how no-ble free-dom was won.

00862507

THE CHANUKKAH SONG

Band Arrangement

Arranged by MICHAEL SWEENEY

00862507

Music and Lyrics by JOHNNY MARKS
Arranged by MICHAEL SWEENEY

Solo

A HOLLY JOLLY CHRISTMAS

Music and Lyrics by JOHNNY MARKS
Arranged by MICHAEL SWEENEY

Band Arrangement

WE WISH YOU A MERRY CHRISTMAS

Solo

Arranged by MICHAEL SWEENEY

WE WISH YOU A MERRY CHRISTMAS

Band Arrangement

Arranged by MICHAEL SWEENEY

00862507

FROSTY THE SNOWMAN

Words and Music by STEVE NELSON and JACK ROLLINS

Arranged by MICHAEL SWEENEY

Solo

FROSTY THE SNOWMAN

Words and Music by STEVE NELSON and JACK ROLLINS
Arranged by MICHAEL SWEENEY

Band Arrangement

ROCKIN' AROUND THE CHRISTMAS TREE

Music and Lyrics by JOHNNY MARKS
Arranged by MICHAEL SWEENEY

ROCKIN' AROUND THE CHRISTMAS TREE

Music and Lyrics by JOHNNY MARKS
Arranged by MICHAEL SWEENEY

Band Arrangement

JINGLE-BELL ROCK

Words and Music by JOE BEAL and JIM BOOTHE
Arranged by MICHAEL SWEENEY

Solo

Jin-gle-bell, Jin-gle-bell, Jin-gle-bell rock Jin-gle-bell swing and Jin-gle-bells ring. Snow-in' and blow-in' up bush-els of fun Now the Jin-gle-hop has be-gun. Jin-gle-bell, Jin-gle-bell, Jin-gle-bell rock Jin-gle-bells chime in Jin-gle-bell time. Danc-in' and pranc-in' in Jin-gle-bell Square In the frost-y air. What a bright time, it's the right time to rock the night a-way. Jin-gle-bell time is a swell time to go glid-in' in a one-horse sleigh. Gid-dy-ap, Jin-gle-horse pick up your feet. Jin-gle a-round the clock. Mix and min-gle in a jin-gl-in' beat. That's the Jin-gle-bell, That's the Jin-gle-bell, That's the Jin-gle-bell rock.

JINGLE-BELL ROCK

**Words and Music by JOE BEAL
and JIM BOOTHE**
Arranged by MICHAEL SWEENEY

Band Arrangement

00862507

RUDOLPH THE RED-NOSED REINDEE

Music and Lyrics by JOHNNY MARKS

Arranged by MICHAEL SWEENEY

Solo

Music and Lyrics by JOHNNY MARKS
Arranged by MICHAEL SWEENEY

Band Arrangement

LET IT SNOW!
Let It Snow! Let It Snow!

Words by SAMMY CAHN
Music by JULE STYNE
Arranged by MICHAEL SWEENEY

Solo

Oh the weath-er out-side is fright-ful But the fire is so de-light-ful, And since we've no place to go, Let it snow! Let it snow! Let it snow! It does-n't show signs of stop-ping, And I brought some corn for pop-ping, The lights are turned way down low, Let it snow! Let it snow! Let it snow! When we fi-nal-ly kiss good-night, How I'll hate go-ing out in the storm! But if you'll real-ly hold me tight, All the way home I'll be warm. The fire is slow-ly dy-ing And my dear we're still good-bye-ing, But as long as you love me so, Let it snow! Let it snow! Let it snow! When we snow!

LET IT SNOW! LET IT SNOW! LET IT SNOW!

Words by SAMMY CAHN
Music by JULE STYNE
Arranged by MICHAEL SWEENEY

Band Arrangement

00862507

THE CHRISTMAS SONG

Music and Lyric by MEL TORME and ROBERT WELLS
Arranged by MICHAEL SWEENEY

Solo

T ᴇ ᴄ ᴛ. ᴄ ɴ

Music and Lyric by MEL TORME and ROBERT WELLS

Band Arrangement

Arranged by MICHAEL SWEENEY

00862507